Rediscovering You:

Exploring Sexual Orientation and Gender Identity as an Established Adult

Written by Christa McCrorie, LICSW-S

Acknowledgements

Thank you to my husband, Carl, who helps me live my dreams and loves me unconditionally.

Thank you to my clients-your resilience inspires me every day.

Thank you to my good friend Jermaine Wall for encouraging me to try things I never dared.

Thank you to Dr. Elizabeth Guthrie, who let me lean on their publishing experience.

Thank you to collaborators on this project, including G. Mansheim, David Roby, Anna Warner, Brantley Ingram, Dr. Andrew Duxbury, and members of ALSAIGE.

Table of Contents

Conclusion

Conclusion of the Workbook

Additional Resources

Introduction

Exploring gender identity and sexual orientation can be a profoundly rewarding journey, yet it often comes with unique challenges, particularly for established adults. Many individuals in this demographic may have spent years conforming to societal expectations or adhering to traditional norms, leaving little room for self-exploration. As we grow older, we may feel pressure to fit into predefined roles or to maintain the status quo, making it harder to question our identities and desires.

For many, the fear of judgment, rejection, or misunderstanding can create significant barriers to authentic self-expression. Life experiences, familial expectations, and societal norms can lead to internalized beliefs that discourage open exploration of one's true self. As established adults, we may grapple with feelings of uncertainty, anxiety, or guilt when considering the possibility of redefining our identities, leaving many feeling isolated in their journey.

I am Christa McCrorie, LICSW-S, a therapist who specializes in queer needs in my own therapy private practice, Creative Therapeutic Solutions, LLC, based in Birmingham, Alabama. I understand these complexities and am dedicated to making the exploration of gender identity and sexual orientation accessible to everyone. My goal is to provide a supportive and affirming space where individuals can freely engage in self-reflection and discover their authentic selves. This workbook is designed to facilitate that process, offering structured activities and journaling prompts that encourage you to delve into your thoughts and feelings.

In this workbook, you will find a variety of tools to help you navigate your identity in a way that feels safe and empowering. Whether you are just beginning your journey of exploration or seeking to deepen your understanding, this resource is here to guide you. Remember, it is never too late to embark on a journey of self-discovery, and you deserve the space and support to explore your unique identity fully. Together, let's embrace this journey with curiosity and compassion, celebrating the beauty of being true to ourselves.

If you are looking to learn more or need individualized support, please reach out to me at:

Creative Therapeutic Solutions, LLC

PO Box 360763, Hoover, AL 35236

Phone: (205) 578-2692

christa.mccrorie@therapysecure.com

https://creativetherapeutic.solutions/

Purpose of the Workbook

The purpose of this workbook is to provide a safe and supportive space for individuals to explore their gender identity and sexual orientation. Through a series of reflective activities, journaling prompts, and creative exercises, this workbook aims to:

1. Facilitate Self-Discovery: Encourage individuals to delve into their thoughts, feelings, and experiences related to their gender identity and sexual orientation, fostering a deeper understanding of themselves.

2. Promote Affirmation and Acceptance: Help individuals recognize and affirm their unique identities, empowering them to embrace their authentic selves without fear of judgment or societal expectations.

3. Encourage Reflection: Provide structured opportunities for reflection, allowing individuals to process their experiences, challenges, and growth in a meaningful way.

4. Foster Community and Connection: Highlight the importance of community and support, encouraging individuals to seek connection with others who share similar experiences and journeys.

5. Provide Resources for Ongoing Exploration: Offer additional resources, affirmations, and support options to guide individuals as they continue to navigate their identities beyond the workbook.

6. Empower Personal Growth: Inspire individuals to set personal goals, celebrate their progress, and cultivate self-compassion, ultimately promoting a healthier and more fulfilling relationship with themselves and their identities.

By engaging with this workbook, individuals can embark on a transformative journey of self-exploration, leading to greater self-awareness, acceptance, and empowerment in their gender identity and sexual orientation.

How to Use This Workbook

Welcome to your journey of self-discovery! This workbook is designed to help you explore your gender identity and sexual orientation in a supportive and affirming way. Here's how to get the most out of this resource:

1. Set the Stage

   - Find a Comfortable Space: Choose a quiet, comfortable place where you can reflect without distractions. This could be a cozy corner of your home, a park, or anywhere you feel safe and at ease.

   - Gather Your Materials: Have your workbook, a journal or notebook, pens or pencils, and any art supplies you might want to use for creative activities.

2. Read the Introduction

   - Start by reading the introduction to understand the purpose of the workbook and the importance of exploring your identity. Familiarize yourself with the affirmations and support resources provided to remind yourself of your worth throughout this journey.

3. Follow the Structure

   - The workbook is divided into sections focused on various aspects of gender identity and sexual orientation. Each section contains activities and journaling prompts.

   - It is recommended to work through the sections in order, as they build upon one another. However, feel free to revisit any section that resonates with you.

4. Engage Fully with Each Activity

   - Reflect and Respond: Take your time with each activity and journaling prompt. Write down your thoughts, feelings, and insights without holding back. There are no right or wrong answers—only your personal truth.

   - Be Creative: Use drawings, collages, or other creative expressions if that feels more comfortable than writing. Let your imagination flow!

5. Take Breaks as Needed

   - If you find yourself feeling overwhelmed or emotional, it's perfectly okay to take a break. Step away from the workbook for a little while and return when you're ready.

6. Practice Self-Compassion

   - As you explore your identity, be gentle with yourself. It's normal to encounter difficult feelings and uncertainties. Remember the affirmations and support resources to help you navigate these emotions.

7. Reflect on Your Progress

   - At the end of each section, take a moment to reflect on what you've learned about yourself. Consider keeping a separate journal to track your thoughts and progress over time.

8. Seek Support if Needed

   - If you feel comfortable, share your insights or experiences with trusted friends, family, or support groups. Engaging with others can enhance your understanding and provide additional perspectives.

9. Celebrate Your Journey

   - Recognize and celebrate the progress you make throughout this workbook. Whether it's gaining new insights, discovering affirming language, or connecting with your identity, every step is significant.

10. Continue the Exploration

   - After completing the workbook, continue exploring your gender identity and sexual orientation. Consider revisiting sections that resonate with you or engaging in new resources, workshops, or community events.

A note on repetition: You may notice that some of these activities and journal prompts may be somewhat repetitive. This is because these activties and journal prompts are meant to be considered over and over again! As you will learn in this workbook, exploring gender identity and sexual orientation can be cyclic in nature, and change over time. The more you discover, the more there is to explore! So, some of these activties and journal prompts are similar to previous ones in the workbook to offer the opportunity to the reader to ask these questions again as they learn more about themselves.

A note on combining gender identity and sexual orientation: Although this book is separated into several parts, one part focusing on gender identity exploration and another part focusing on sexual orientation, you will often find throughout this workbook that each part will reference the other. This is because defining gender identity and sexual orientation are rarely separate processes, but rather exploring either of these is discovering a greater experience of queerness individual to each person. While some people using this workbook may only define elements of their gender identity or sexual orientation but not both, others may explore and define both elements into discovering their own queer experience.

Ground Rules for Reflection and Exploration

1. Confidentiality is Key

Respect the privacy of your thoughts and reflections. What you share in this space stays in this space.

2. Be Honest with Yourself

Allow yourself to express your true feelings and thoughts without judgment. Honesty is crucial for genuine self-exploration.

3. Practice Self-Compassion

Treat yourself with kindness and understanding as you navigate complex emotions and experiences. Remember, it's okay to feel uncertain.

4. No Right or Wrong Answers

Understand that there are no correct responses. Everyone's journey is unique, and all feelings and experiences are valid.

5. Take Your Time

Allow yourself to engage with the activities and prompts at your own pace. There's no rush; this is your personal journey.

6. Avoid Comparisons

Focus on your own experiences without comparing them to others. Each person's journey is different, and that diversity should be celebrated.

7. Embrace Vulnerability

Be open to sharing your thoughts and feelings, even if it feels uncomfortable. Vulnerability can lead to greater understanding and growth.

8. Set Boundaries

If certain topics or questions feel too personal or triggering, it's okay to skip them or take a break. Honor your boundaries.

9. Seek Support When Needed

If you find yourself feeling overwhelmed, consider reaching out to a trusted friend, counselor, or support group for assistance.

10. Celebrate Your Progress

Acknowledge the steps you take, no matter how small. Each reflection and exploration contributes to your growth and understanding.

11. Use Affirming Language

Be mindful of the language you use when reflecting on your identity. Affirming language can foster a positive self-image.

12. Stay Open-Minded

Approach each prompt and activity with an open mind. Be willing to explore new ideas and perspectives about yourself.

13. Engage in Active Listening

If discussing with others, practice active listening. Respect others' experiences and insights without judgment.

14. Reflect Regularly

Make time for regular reflection beyond the workbook activities. Ongoing self-reflection can deepen your understanding and awareness.

15. Have Fun

Remember that this exploration can be a joyful and enlightening process. Allow yourself to enjoy the journey of self-discovery.

Affirmations and Support Resources

As you go through this workbook, you may be met with uncomfortable feelings. Here are some affirmations to help ground you in facing these uncomfortable feelings, and additional support resources for overwhelming, violent, self-harm, or suicidal feelings. If you are having thoughts of hurting yourself or another person, call 911 or go to the nearest emergency room. At the end of this workbook, there are more resources to learn more about exploring your queer identity.

Affirmations for Gender Identity and Sexual Orientation Exploration

1. I am worthy of love and acceptance, just as I am.

2. My feelings and experiences are valid and deserving of exploration.

3. I embrace my unique identity and celebrate my journey of self-discovery.

4. It is okay to question and explore my gender identity and sexual orientation.

5. I have the right to express my identity in ways that feel authentic to me.

6. I am not alone; there is a supportive community ready to embrace me.

7. My identity is not defined by others' perceptions; it is defined by my truth.

8. I am proud of my journey and the courage it takes to be myself.

9. It's okay to change and evolve; growth is a natural part of life.

10. I choose to surround myself with supportive and affirming people.

11. My identity is a beautiful and unique expression of who I am.

12. I deserve to be treated with respect and dignity in all spaces.

13. I will advocate for myself and seek the support I need.

14. I honor my feelings and experiences, even when they are challenging.

15. I am deserving of joy and fulfillment in my relationships and life.

Support Resources

1. Online Communities and Forums

- Reddit: LGBTQ+ Community

A supportive online community where individuals can share experiences, ask questions, and find advice.

www.reddit.com/r/lgbt

- The Trevor Project

 A crisis intervention and suicide prevention organization for LGBTQ+ youth, providing support through chat, text, and phone.

 www.thetrevorproject.org

- LGBTQ+ Support Groups on Facebook

 Search for local or online support groups for LGBTQ+ individuals to connect and share experiences.

2. Hotlines and Crisis Support

- Trevor Lifeline

 A confidential hotline for LGBTQ+ youth in crisis. Available 24/7.

 Phone: 1-866-488-7386

- GLBT National Help Center

 Provides free and confidential support via phone and chat for LGBTQ+ individuals.

 Phone: 1-888-843-4564

 www.glbthotline.org

- Trans Lifeline

 A peer support service for the transgender community, offering emotional support.

 Phone: 1-877-565-8860

 www.translifeline.org

3. Books and Literature

- The Gendered Self by R.W. Connell

 Explores the concept of gender and identity from a sociological perspective.

- Gender Outlaws: The Next Generation edited by Kate Bornstein and S. Bear Bergman

A collection of essays by various authors discussing gender identity and expression.

- Becoming Nicole: The Transformation of an American Family by Amy Ellis Nutt

A true story about a transgender girl and her family's journey toward acceptance.

4. Educational Resources and Websites

- PFLAG

An organization that offers support, education, and advocacy for LGBTQ+ individuals and their families.

www.pflag.org

- GLAAD

An organization that promotes LGBTQ+ acceptance and provides resources for allies.

www.glaad.org

- The Human Rights Campaign (HRC)

Provides resources, advocacy, and support for LGBTQ+ rights.

www.hrc.org

5. Local Support Organizations

- Find Your Local LGBTQ+ Center

Many cities have local LGBTQ+ centers that offer support groups, counseling, and resources. Search for local resources through the following:

www.lgbtcenters.org

- Counseling Services

Look for therapists or counselors specializing in LGBTQ+ issues in your area. Many provide affirming care for individuals exploring their gender identity and sexual orientation.

6. Workshops and Events

- LGBTQ+ Community Events

  Look for local Pride events, workshops, and community gatherings to connect with others. Check local community centers or LGBTQ+ organizations for upcoming events.

- Online Webinars and Workshops

  Many organizations offer online workshops focused on gender identity and sexual orientation. Search for offerings from local LGBTQ+ organizations or national advocacy groups.

Section 1: Understanding Gender Identity

Exploring gender identity is a deeply personal and often transformative process that can significantly impact an individual's sense of self and overall well-being. For established adults, meaning adults who have already settled into their life, perhaps with their career, partner, living situation, religious community, children, or other roles that deeply define their self, this journey may be particularly complex. Many adults have spent years adhering to societal norms and expectations regarding gender roles and sexual orientation. As a result, questioning one's identity later in life can evoke a mixture of excitement and anxiety, as well as feelings of confusion, self-doubt, and grief.

The Nature of Gender Identity

Gender identity refers to an individual's internal sense of their own gender, which may align with the sex assigned to them at birth or differ from it. It encompasses a spectrum of identities, including but not limited to male, female, transgender, non-binary, genderqueer, and genderfluid. Understanding this spectrum is essential for recognizing the diversity of experiences that individuals may encounter in their journey of self-exploration.

For many adults, the process of discovering or affirming their gender identity involves a re-examination of the beliefs, norms, and expectations they have internalized over the years. This introspective journey can prompt individuals to confront the limitations imposed by societal norms and challenge the binary understanding of gender. Engaging in this exploration allows individuals to connect with their authentic selves and embrace their unique identities.

Challenges and Barriers

While the journey of self-exploration can be rewarding, it often presents several challenges. Established adults may face internalized fears about societal rejection, stigmatization, or a lack of understanding from family and friends. The pressure to conform to traditional gender roles can create significant stress and anxiety, leading individuals to question their desires and identity.

Furthermore, individuals may grapple with the implications of coming out, such as changes in relationships, potential backlash from their communities, or even feelings of isolation. These fears can create a barrier to self-acceptance and inhibit honest exploration of one's identity. Recognizing and addressing these challenges is an important part of the journey.

The Importance of Community and Support

Throughout this exploration, the role of community and support cannot be overstated. Engaging with others who share similar experiences can provide validation, encouragement, and a sense of belonging. Support from friends, family, or LGBTQ+ groups can create a safe space for individuals to express themselves freely without judgment. Finding a supportive network is essential for fostering resilience and facilitating open conversations about identity.

As you embark on your journey, it is vital to seek out spaces where you feel comfortable expressing your thoughts and feelings. Whether through local community events, online forums, or support groups, connecting with others can help you navigate the complexities of your exploration and provide insights into the diverse ways people understand and experience gender.

Embracing Fluidity and Change

An important aspect of exploring gender identity is recognizing that identity can be fluid and dynamic. For many individuals, gender identity is not a fixed label but rather an evolving understanding of oneself. Embracing this fluidity allows for a more authentic exploration and encourages individuals to engage in ongoing self-discovery.

As you reflect on your identity, be open to the possibility that your understanding of yourself may change over time. Allowing for this evolution can lead to deeper self-acceptance and an enriched understanding of who you are. Your journey is uniquely yours, and it is essential to honor and celebrate your individual experiences along the way.

The Spectrum of LGBTQ+ Identities

The LGBTQ+ community encompasses a wide range of identities and expressions that reflect the rich diversity of human experience. Here are some key spectrums within the LGBTQ+ umbrella:

1. Sexual Orientation

   - Lesbian: Women who are attracted to women.

   - Gay: Men who are attracted to men, though it can also refer to individuals of any gender attracted to the same gender.

   - Bisexual: Individuals who are attracted to both men and women.

- Pansexual: Individuals who are attracted to people regardless of their gender identity, emphasizing attraction to the person rather than their gender.

- Asexual: Individuals who experience little or no sexual attraction to others, though they may still desire romantic relationships.

2. Gender Identity

- Cisgender: Individuals whose gender identity aligns with the sex they were assigned at birth.

- Transgender: Individuals whose gender identity differs from the sex assigned to them at birth. This spectrum can include those who identify as male or female and those who may identify outside the traditional binary.

- Non-Binary: Individuals who do not exclusively identify as male or female. This can encompass a variety of identities, such as genderqueer, genderfluid, or agender, each reflecting different experiences and expressions of gender.

- Genderqueer: A term used by some individuals who reject traditional gender categories and may identify with aspects of multiple genders.

3. Gender Expression

- Gender Expression: Refers to how an individual presents their gender to the outside world through clothing, behavior, hairstyle, voice, and more. Gender expression can be masculine, feminine, androgynous, or anything in between, and it may not necessarily align with an individual's gender identity.

4. Intersectionality

- Recognizing that individuals exist at the intersection of multiple identities is crucial. Factors such as race, ethnicity, socioeconomic status, ability, and cultural background can influence experiences within the LGBTQ+ community, highlighting the need for an intersectional approach to understanding identity.

A Note: Language around LGBTQ+ spectrums and communities are always changing, so these identifiers listed here are meant to be a beginning point in your understanding.

Theories of Identity Development

Many people who are exploring their gender identity and sexual orientation as an adult may have come from cultural, political, or religious backgrounds that invalidate the experience of LGBTQ+ people. Below are listed several development theories of LGBTQ+ experiences to normalize the developmental experiences of LGBTQ+ people. These theories are broad, and are meant to be a jumping off point to explore other theories in other contexts.

Istar Lev Model of Transgender Emergence

The Istar Lev Model of Transgender Emergence, made by Arlene Istar Lev, is a comprehensive framework for understanding the process of transgender identity development. This model includes several key steps: Awareness, where individuals begin to recognize their gender dysphoria; Seeking Information/Reaching Out, where they explore transgender identities and seek out resources; Disclosure to Significant Others, where they begin to share their identity with close friends and family; Exploration of Identity and Transition, where they experiment with gender expression and may begin medical or social transition; and Integration, where they fully embrace their transgender identity and integrate it into their overall sense of self, leading to a sense of authenticity and self-acceptance.

The Transgender Emergence Model developed by Arlene Istar Lev outlines six key stages in the process of transgender identity development. Here are the six steps:

1. Awareness: This stage involves the initial recognition of feelings of gender dysphoria or a sense that one's gender identity does not align with the sex assigned at birth.

2. Seeking Information/Reaching Out: In this stage, individuals begin to explore transgender identities, seeking out information, resources, and support from others who may share similar experiences.

3. Disclosure to Significant Others: During this step, individuals start to share their gender identity with close friends, family members, or significant others. This can involve discussing their feelings, experiences, and possibly their plans for transition.

4. Exploration of Identity and Transition: This stage includes experimenting with gender expression, such as clothing, name changes, or pronouns, and may involve beginning a social, medical, or legal transition.

5. Integration: At this point, individuals work to integrate their transgender identity into their overall sense of self. This involves reconciling their gender identity with other aspects of their life and finding a sense of authenticity and self-acceptance.

6. Pride: In this final stage, individuals embrace their transgender identity fully and may become more active in advocacy or the transgender community. This stage is marked by a strong sense of pride in one's identity and achievements.

These stages provide a framework for understanding the complex journey of transgender individuals as they navigate their identity and transition. This model, although originally meant for transgender individuals, can be modified to support and provide a framework for others with gender development considerations.

Vivienne Cass's Model of Homosexual Identity Development

Vivienne Cass's Model of Homosexual Identity Development outlines a six-stage process for individuals coming to recognize and integrate a homosexual identity. Though originally developed for homosexual identity, this model has been adapted for understanding the identity development of LGBTQ+ individuals more broadly. Here's an outline of the model along with steps involved at each stage:

1. Identity Confusion

Description: This is the first stage where the individual begins to question whether they might be gay or lesbian. This often arises due to feelings or attractions that don't align with heterosexual expectations.

Steps:

Experiences initial awareness of same-sex attraction.

Begins to question their sexual identity.

May feel anxiety, confusion, or even denial about this possibility.

2. Identity Comparison

Description: In this stage, the individual starts to consider the implications of being gay, often feeling isolated or different from others. They may compare themselves with others and feel a sense of alienation.

Steps:

Considers the potential consequences of having a homosexual identity.

May experience feelings of alienation or "not fitting in" with heterosexual peers.

Begins to develop an internal dialogue about being "different."

3. Identity Tolerance

Description: The individual begins to accept the possibility of a homosexual identity, often seeking out other gay and lesbian people or communities for support and validation.

Steps:

Moves towards self-acceptance and tolerates the idea of being homosexual.

Begins seeking out LGBTQ+ people or spaces for validation.

May experience a mixture of relief (from connecting with others) and internalized homophobia.

4. Identity Acceptance

Description: At this stage, the individual starts to embrace their homosexual identity more openly and accepts it as part of who they are.

Steps:

Forms stronger connections within the LGBTQ+ community.

May start to disclose their identity to close friends or family.

Experiences a growing sense of pride in their identity, although struggles with social stigma may continue.

5. Identity Pride

Description: The individual fully embraces and takes pride in their homosexual identity, often leading to activism or efforts to confront societal stigma.

Steps:

Experiences a sense of pride in being openly gay or lesbian.

May become outspoken about LGBTQ+ rights and resist heteronormative pressures.

Might struggle with feelings of anger or frustration toward heterosexist structures.

6. Identity Synthesis

Description: In this final stage, the individual integrates their sexual identity with other aspects of themselves, viewing it as one part of their whole identity rather than the defining feature.

Steps:

Achieves a balanced self-concept where being gay or lesbian is one part of a multifaceted identity.

Experiences acceptance of both LGBTQ+ and heterosexual individuals in their social circles.

Finds peace with their identity and is generally comfortable navigating the world authentically.

The Cass model progresses from initial confusion and questioning to a fully integrated identity. It's a non-linear process where individuals may revisit earlier stages based on life circumstances, experiences, and social contexts. The model also emphasizes the importance of self-acceptance, community connection, and pride in reaching a stable and healthy LGBTQ+ identity.

Social Constructionism

Social constructionism views sexual orientation, gender, and other identities as socially constructed rather than biologically fixed traits. This theory emphasizes that social, cultural, and historical contexts play a key role in shaping identities, which can vary across different cultures and time periods. Here's an outline of the core concepts and stages in social constructionist theory:

1. Definition of Social Constructionism

-Description : Social constructionism posits that knowledge, identities, and categories are created through social processes, language, and cultural norms. Rather than being innate, these identities are viewed as constructed through interactions within specific cultural and social contexts.

-Key Point : Emphasizes that sexuality and gender are fluid and changeable, influenced by social and historical forces rather than being purely biological.

2. Role of Language and Discourse

-Description : Language and discourse play a central role in constructing identities by shaping how people understand and categorize experiences.

-Key Point : The words and categories people use (e.g., "gay," "straight," "bisexual") are products of cultural norms and can vary significantly across societies and eras. Language shapes how individuals perceive themselves and others.

3. Historical and Cultural Relativity

-Description : Social constructionism suggests that concepts like sexual orientation are not universal; they differ based on cultural and historical context.

-Key Point : What is considered "normal" or "deviant" changes over time and place. For example, same-sex relationships were normalized in some cultures and stigmatized in others, showing how societal values influence identity.

4. Identity as a Social Product

-Description : Sexual orientation and gender identities are seen as products of societal expectations and cultural interactions.

- Key Point : Identity is not a fixed essence within a person but a social product that can shift based on the individual's environment, social influences, and personal experiences.

5. Fluidity and Variability of Identity

-Description : Social constructionism emphasizes the fluid and flexible nature of identity. People may shift how they identify based on context and personal growth.

-Key Point : Identities are not static; individuals can adopt different labels or orientations over time, reflecting the dynamic and evolving nature of personal identity.

6. Challenge to Essentialism

-Description : Social constructionism challenges essentialist perspectives that suggest identities are biologically or psychologically fixed.

-Key Point : Rather than being inherent traits, identities like sexual orientation are seen as shaped by external social conditions. Essentialist ideas (e.g., that people are "born gay" or "born straight") are critiqued as oversimplifications.

7. Queer Theory and Deconstruction of Categories

-Description : Queer theory, a branch of social constructionism, deconstructs traditional categories of sexuality and gender, arguing that rigid labels are restrictive.

-Key Point : Queer theorists advocate for moving beyond binaries (like gay/straight or male/female) and embracing a broader, more inclusive understanding of identity that allows for fluidity and multiplicity.

The social constructionist approach highlights that sexual orientation and identity are products of social, cultural, and historical processes rather than intrinsic qualities. It emphasizes the roles of language, cultural context, and fluidity, challenging essentialist views and promoting an understanding of identity as adaptable and evolving over time. This approach has been influential in LGBTQ+ studies, sociology, and gender theory, as it encourages a more nuanced view of identity formation.

The Path Ahead

This workbook is designed to guide you through the exploration of your gender identity and sexual orientation. By engaging with the activities and journal prompts included in this section, you can begin to reflect on your thoughts, feelings, and experiences. The goal is to provide you with tools to navigate your journey, helping you gain clarity and insight into your identity.

Through this process, you will have the opportunity to explore your cultural background, challenge societal norms, express your emotions creatively, and connect with supportive communities. Each activity is an invitation to delve deeper into your self-discovery, allowing you to uncover the layers of your identity and embrace your authentic self.

As you embark on this journey, remember that you are not alone. Many have walked this path before you, and there is a vibrant community of individuals who share similar experiences and insights. Embrace the exploration ahead, and allow yourself the grace to discover who you truly are.

Journal Prompt:

-How has the idea of gender identity and sexual orientation changed over time in my culture? In my religious group? In politics?

-How has my own gender identity and sexual orientation changed over my lifetime?

-How do I feel about starting to explore my gender identity and sexual orientation?

Understanding gender identity and sexual orientation within cultural contexts is crucial for individuals on their journey of self-exploration. Each culture has its own historical, social, and political frameworks that shape the experiences of LGBTQ+ individuals. These frameworks can significantly influence how identities are perceived, accepted, and expressed.

Different cultures may have unique terms and understandings for gender and sexuality that do not always align with Western definitions. This diversity highlights the importance of recognizing and respecting varied cultural perspectives as you explore your own identity.

Indigenous and Non-Western Cultures

Many indigenous cultures have long recognized and embraced a spectrum of gender identities beyond the binary framework commonly found in Western societies. For example:

- Two-Spirit: In many Native American cultures, the term Two-Spirit describes individuals who embody both masculine and feminine qualities. This concept reflects a deep spiritual connection to both genders and often includes roles in community leadership, healing, and ceremony. Two-Spirit individuals may experience a unique sense of identity that combines both their gender identity and cultural heritage.

- Hijra: In South Asian cultures, particularly in India and Pakistan, hijras are recognized as a distinct third gender. Traditionally, hijras have occupied specific social roles, often serving as performers at weddings and childbirth ceremonies. While hijra identity can encompass transgender and intersex individuals, their cultural significance and societal roles can vary widely.

- Fa'afafine: In Samoan culture, fa'afafine are individuals assigned male at birth who embody both male and female gender traits. This identity is widely accepted within Samoan society, and fa'afafine often play important roles in family and community life, challenging traditional Western binary notions of gender.

LGBTQ+ Identities in Global Contexts

Across the globe, LGBTQ+ identities are influenced by cultural beliefs, religious practices, and political climates. Here are a few examples of how LGBTQ+ identities manifest in different cultural contexts:

- Latin American Cultures: In many Latin American countries, traditional gender roles and machismo culture can create challenges for LGBTQ+ individuals. However, countries like Mexico have a vibrant LGBTQ+ community, with cities like Mexico City celebrating pride events and activism. In contrast, some Central American nations have restrictive laws against LGBTQ+ rights, making the experiences of LGBTQ+ individuals vastly different across the region.

- Middle Eastern Cultures: In many Middle Eastern countries, LGBTQ+ identities face significant social stigma and legal challenges. However, there are also underground LGBTQ+ communities that find ways to express their identities. For instance, in Lebanon, there has been a burgeoning LGBTQ+ rights movement, despite the legal and social obstacles faced by queer individuals.

- Asian Cultures: LGBTQ+ identities in Asian cultures can be diverse and complex. In Japan, while traditional gender roles have historically prevailed, the presence of queer literature, art, and activism is growing. On the other hand, in countries like China, discussions around LGBTQ+ rights are becoming more visible, but individuals may still face cultural pressure to conform to heteronormative expectations.

Intersectionality and Cultural Nuances

Cultural context also intersects with other aspects of identity, such as race, ethnicity, religion, and socioeconomic status. For instance, Black queer individuals may experience unique challenges and forms of discrimination that are distinct from those faced by their white counterparts, even within the LGBTQ+ community. Understanding the intersections of these identities is essential for recognizing the diversity of experiences among LGBTQ+ individuals.

As you reflect on your own identity, consider how your cultural background influences your understanding of gender and sexuality. Recognizing the role of culture in shaping identities can deepen your exploration and foster a greater appreciation for the diversity of human experiences.

The Path Ahead

This section aims to encourage you to reflect on the cultural factors that shape your understanding of gender identity and sexual orientation. As you engage with the activities and journal prompts in this workbook, consider how cultural beliefs and practices may have influenced your experiences and perceptions.

By honoring your unique cultural context and acknowledging the diversity of LGBTQ+ identities across the globe, you can cultivate a more nuanced understanding of your identity and the identities of others. This awareness will enrich your journey of self-discovery, allowing you to embrace the complexity and richness of your own experience while fostering empathy and connection with others.

Journal Prompt:

- How has my cultural background influenced my understanding of gender and sexuality?

- What societal norms have I internalized regarding gender and sexual orientation, and how do they impact my self-perception?

Conclusion

The journey of self-exploration is complex and multifaceted. For many adults, it involves confronting societal expectations, internalized biases, and the fear of judgment from others. It is essential to recognize that this process is not linear; it may include moments of clarity, confusion, joy, and discomfort.

Interactive Challenges

Engaging in interactive challenges can be an effective way to deepen your understanding of your gender identity and sexual orientation. These activities encourage self-reflection, creativity, and connection with others, making the journey of exploration both enlightening and enjoyable. Here are some interactive challenges you can undertake as part of your self-discovery process:

1. Identity Mapping

Objective: Visualize and explore the different facets of your identity.

Instructions:

- Use the next page to draw your mind map.

- In the center of the page, write My Identity and surround it with branches representing various aspects of who you are (e.g., gender, sexual orientation, cultural background, hobbies, and values).

- For each branch, add specific words, images, or symbols that resonate with that aspect of your identity.

- Reflect on how these components interact and shape your overall sense of self.

Draw Your Mind Map Below:

Reflection Questions:

- How do these aspects of your identity influence each other?

- Are there identities you wish to explore further?

---

2. Letter to Your Future Self

Objective: Express your current thoughts and feelings while envisioning your future.

Instructions:

- Write a letter on the next page addressed to your future self, describing your current understanding of your gender identity and sexual orientation.

- Include your hopes, dreams, and any challenges you foresee facing.

- Seal the letter and set a date to open it in the future (e.g., six months or a year).

Write a Letter to Yourself Below:

Reflection Questions:

- What insights did you gain while writing this letter?

- How do you hope your understanding of your identity will evolve over time?

____
____
____
____
____
____
____
____
____
____
____
____

3. Role-Playing Scenarios

Objective: Practice navigating conversations about your identity in a safe space.

Instructions:

- Pair up with a trusted friend or support group member. Take turns role-playing scenarios where you might need to discuss your gender identity or sexual orientation.

- One person can act as a supportive friend, while the other practices expressing their feelings or responding to questions. Switch roles after a few scenarios.

- If you're comfortable, you can also include scenarios where the conversation may be challenging, allowing you to practice assertiveness and boundary-setting.

Reflection Questions:

- How did it feel to express your identity in these scenarios?

- Were there any challenges you encountered? How might you address them in real life?

____
____
____
____
____
____
____
____
____
____

4. Creative Expression

Objective: Use artistic outlets to express your identity and feelings.

Instructions:

- Choose a creative medium that resonates with you, such as painting, drawing, writing poetry, or creating a collage.

- Use the next piece of paper to create a piece that represents your gender identity, sexual orientation, or journey of self-discovery. Allow yourself to explore and experiment without judgment.

- If you feel comfortable, share your creation with a friend or in a supportive group setting.

Make Art Here:

Reflection Questions:

- What emotions surfaced during the creative process?

- How does your artwork reflect your understanding of your identity?

____
____
____
____
____
____
____
____
____

5. Find Your Community

Objective: Explore local and online communities that resonate with your identity.

Instructions:

- Research LGBTQ+ organizations, support groups, and events in your area or online. Consider factors such as inclusivity, focus areas, and community values.

- Attend a local LGBTQ+ event, join an online forum, or participate in a workshop that aligns with your interests. Engage with others and share your experiences.

Reflection Questions:

- What did you learn from connecting with others in these communities?

- How did it feel to share your identity in a supportive space?

____
____
____
____
____
____
____

6. Identity Exploration Journal

Objective: Regularly reflect on your thoughts and experiences related to your identity.

Instructions:

- Dedicate a journal (outside of this one!) specifically to exploring your gender identity and sexual orientation. Write entries regularly, focusing on different aspects of your identity, feelings, and experiences.

- You can include prompts such as: What does being [insert identity] mean to me? or What challenges do I face in expressing my identity?

Reflection Questions:

- How has journaling impacted your understanding of your identity?

- What themes or patterns have emerged in your entries?

____
____
____
____
____
____
____
____
____
____
____

7. Affirmation Challenge

Objective: Cultivate self-love and acceptance through positive affirmations.

Instructions:

- Create a list of affirmations on the next page that resonate with your journey of self-discovery (e.g., I am worthy of love and acceptance or My identity is valid and important).

- Choose a time each day to read these affirmations aloud or write them in your journal.

- Challenge yourself to create new affirmations based on your evolving understanding of your identity.

Write Affirmations Here:

1. ____

2. ____

3. ____

4. ____

5. ____

6. ____

7. ____

8. ____

9. ____

10. ____

11. ____

12. ____

13. ____

14. ____

15. ____

16. ____

17. ____

18. ____

19. ____

20. ____

Reflection Questions:

- How do these affirmations make you feel about yourself?

- In what ways can you incorporate affirmations into your daily life?

____
____
____
____
____

Mindfulness and Grounding Techniques

Mindfulness and grounding techniques are powerful tools that can help individuals cultivate self-awareness, manage anxiety, and create a sense of stability during the exploration of their gender identity and sexual orientation. As you navigate the complexities of this journey, incorporating mindfulness practices into your daily routine can foster a deeper connection to yourself and promote a greater sense of well-being.

Understanding Mindfulness

Mindfulness is the practice of paying attention to the present moment without judgment. It involves observing your thoughts, feelings, and bodily sensations with curiosity and compassion. By practicing mindfulness, you can create space to acknowledge your emotions and experiences without becoming overwhelmed by them. This awareness can be especially beneficial during times of uncertainty or self-discovery, allowing you to approach your journey with an open mind.

Benefits of Mindfulness in Identity Exploration

1. Increased Self-Awareness: Mindfulness encourages self-reflection, helping you to understand your feelings, thoughts, and behaviors more deeply. This increased awareness can aid in identifying and articulating your gender identity and sexual orientation.

2. Stress Reduction: Engaging in mindfulness practices can help reduce anxiety and stress, promoting a sense of calmness. This is particularly important when exploring challenging topics related to identity, as it can create a safe mental space for reflection.

3. Emotional Regulation: Mindfulness allows you to observe your emotions without becoming reactive. This can be valuable when grappling with complex feelings around your identity, helping you respond to situations with greater clarity and intention.

4. Enhanced Acceptance: Mindfulness fosters an attitude of acceptance towards your thoughts and feelings. This acceptance can be liberating as you navigate your identity, allowing you to embrace your experiences without fear of judgment.

Grounding Techniques for Stability

Grounding techniques are practices that help anchor you in the present moment, especially during times of distress or anxiety. These techniques can be particularly useful when exploring your identity, as they provide a sense of safety and stability amid the emotional ups and downs of the journey.

1. 5-4-3-2-1 Grounding Exercise: This technique engages your senses to bring you back to the present moment.

   - 5: Identify five things you can see around you.

   - 4: Identify four things you can touch or feel (e.g., the texture of your clothing, the surface of a chair).

   - 3: Identify three things you can hear (e.g., birds chirping, cars passing).

   - 2: Identify two things you can smell (e.g., fresh coffee, flowers).

   - 1: Identify one thing you can taste (e.g., water, a snack).

This exercise can help redirect your focus and reduce feelings of overwhelm.

Journal or draw the before and aftereffects of this experience

Before: *After:*

2. Breath Awareness: Taking a few moments to focus on your breath can ground you in the present moment.

   - Find a comfortable seated position and close your eyes if it feels safe.

   - Inhale deeply through your nose for a count of four, hold for a count of four, and exhale slowly through your mouth for a count of six.

   - Repeat this cycle for several minutes, allowing your breath to guide you into a state of relaxation.

Journal or draw the before and after effects of this experience

Before: *After:*

3. Body Scan: This technique encourages awareness of physical sensations and promotes relaxation.

   - Lie down or sit comfortably, close your eyes, and take a few deep breaths.

   - Starting from the top of your head, slowly bring your attention to each part of your body, noticing any sensations or tension.

   - As you move down your body, consciously relax each area, allowing any stress or discomfort to dissipate.

Journal or draw the before and after effects of this experience

Before: *After:*

4. Nature Connection: Engaging with nature can provide grounding and a sense of calm.

   - Take a walk outside and observe your surroundings. Pay attention to the colors, sounds, and smells.

   - If you can, sit on the grass or find a natural setting where you can connect with the earth. Imagine the ground supporting you and absorbing any tension or anxiety.

Journal or draw the before and after effects of this experience

Before:	*After:*

5. Mindful Journaling: Writing can serve as a grounding technique, allowing you to express your thoughts and feelings.

   - Set aside time to write in a journal, focusing on your experiences and reflections related to your identity.

   - Use prompts such as What do I feel today? or What aspects of my identity am I embracing? to guide your writing.

Journal or draw the before and after effects of this experience

Before:	*After:*

Incorporating Mindfulness into Daily Life

If you want to make mindfulness a part of your exploration, here are some practices you can integrate into your daily routine:

- Set Aside Time: Dedicate specific times each day or week to practice mindfulness or grounding techniques. This could be during your morning routine, lunch breaks, or before bedtime.

- Create a Mindfulness Space: Designate a quiet space in your home where you can engage in mindfulness practices. Fill it with calming objects, such as plants, candles, or photographs that inspire you.

- Be Gentle with Yourself: Remember that mindfulness is a practice, and it's okay if your mind wanders or if you find it challenging at times. Approach your practice with self-compassion, allowing yourself the space to grow and learn.

The Path Ahead

As you explore your gender identity and sexual orientation, integrating mindfulness and grounding techniques can provide valuable support along the way. By cultivating awareness and grounding yourself in the present moment, you can navigate the complexities of your journey with greater clarity, resilience, and acceptance.

Incorporating these practices into your routine not only enhances your self-exploration but also fosters a deeper connection to yourself and your experiences. Embrace the journey ahead, and allow mindfulness to be a guiding companion as you uncover the richness of your identity.

Artistic Expression Prompts

Artistic expression serves as a powerful tool for self-discovery and exploration, allowing individuals to convey complex feelings and experiences that might be difficult to articulate through words alone. Engaging in creative activities can provide a sense of freedom and release, facilitating deeper reflection on your gender identity and sexual orientation. Below are various artistic prompts to inspire your exploration and encourage you to express your authentic self.

1. Self-Portrait

Prompt: Create a self-portrait that represents how you see yourself in relation to your gender identity and sexual orientation.

- Instructions: Use any medium you feel comfortable with—drawing, painting, collage, or digital art. Consider incorporating colors, symbols, and images that resonate with your feelings about your identity. Reflect on how you want to represent yourself visually and what elements are essential to conveying your unique experience. You may also use the next page.

Make Self Portrait Here:

Reflection Questions:

- What aspects of your identity did you choose to highlight in your self-portrait?

- How do you feel about the representation of yourself in this artwork?

-Are you satisfied with how you feel looking at your representation? If not, what needs to change?

____
____
____
____
____
____
____
____
____
____

2. Identity Collage

Prompt: Create a collage that represents different aspects of your identity, including your gender identity, sexual orientation, and other elements that shape who you are.

- Instructions: Gather images, words, and materials from magazines, newspapers, or the internet that resonate with your sense of self. Arrange and layer these items on a canvas or piece of paper, allowing your intuition to guide you. Feel free to include personal photographs, meaningful quotes, or objects that hold significance to you. You can use the next page for your collage.

Make Collage Here:

Reflection Questions:

- What themes emerged as you created your collage?

- How do the images and words you selected reflect your identity?

____
____
____
____
____
____
____
____
____
____

3. Storytelling Through Art

Prompt: Use visual storytelling to depict a significant moment in your journey of self-discovery related to your gender identity or sexual orientation.

- Instructions: Choose a moment that stands out to you—whether it's a realization, a coming-out experience, or a pivotal conversation. Create a series of illustrations or a comic strip that narrates this moment. Focus on the emotions, thoughts, and sensory experiences you encountered during that time. Use the next page.

Illustrate Your Story Here:

Reflection Questions:

- What emotions did you feel as you illustrated this moment?

- How does this story contribute to your overall understanding of your identity?

____
____
____
____
____
____
____
____
____
____

4. Affirmation Art

Prompt: Design a piece of art that incorporates positive affirmations related to your identity.

- Instructions: Choose affirmations that resonate with you, such as I am enough, My identity is valid, or I embrace my true self. Create an artwork that visually represents these affirmations, using colors, textures, and patterns that inspire you. This can be a poster, a canvas painting, or even a digital graphic. You can also use the next page.

Make Affirmation Art Here:

Reflection Questions:

- How does creating affirmation art make you feel about yourself?

- What role do affirmations play in your journey of self-acceptance?

____
____
____
____
____
____
____
____
____
____

5. Gender Spectrum Exploration

Prompt: Create a piece that represents your understanding of the gender spectrum and where you see yourself within it.

- Instructions: Use color, shapes, and imagery to illustrate your interpretation of the gender spectrum. You can represent your place on the spectrum through abstract art, a diagram, or a more figurative approach. Allow your creativity to guide you in expressing how you relate to different aspects of gender. You can use the next page.

Illustrate Gender Spectrum:

Reflection Questions:

- What insights did you gain about your relationship to the gender spectrum through this artwork?

- How does this representation reflect your feelings about your identity?

____
____
____
____
____
____
____
____
____
____

6. Sound and Movement

Prompt: Explore your identity through sound and movement by creating a soundscape or movement piece.

- Instructions: Choose music or sounds that resonate with your identity and evoke specific feelings. You can create a playlist that reflects your journey, or if you feel inspired, choreograph a dance or movement sequence that expresses your emotions and experiences related to your identity.

Reflection Questions:

- How did the sounds or movements you chose allow you to express your identity?

- What emotions surfaced during this creative exploration?

____
____
____
____
____
____
____
____
____

7. Poetry or Prose

Prompt: Write a poem or a short prose piece that captures your feelings about your gender identity and sexual orientation.

- Instructions: Allow your thoughts and emotions to flow freely onto the page. You can explore themes such as acceptance, struggle, joy, or transformation. Experiment with different poetic forms or prose styles to find what resonates with you. Write this on the next page.

Write Poetry or Prose Here:

Reflection Questions:

- What emotions did you uncover while writing?

- How does your written piece reflect your journey and identity?

____

____

____

____

____

____

____

____

____

____

8. The Future Self

Prompt: Create a visual representation of your future self as you continue to explore and embrace your gender identity and sexual orientation.

- Instructions: Imagine your future self five or ten years from now. What do you hope to achieve? How do you want to express your identity? Create a piece of art that illustrates this vision, whether it be through a painting, drawing, or digital art. Incorporate elements that symbolize your goals and aspirations. Use the next page.

Visualize the Future Self Below:

Reflection Questions:

- How does envisioning your future self impact your current understanding of your identity?

- What steps can you take today to move towards this vision?

____
____
____
____
____
____
____
____
____
____

Conclusion of Artistic Expression Prompts

Artistic expression offers a unique pathway for exploration and self-discovery. Engaging in these prompts can help you articulate your thoughts, feelings, and experiences related to your gender identity and sexual orientation. Remember, there are no right or wrong ways to create; the purpose is to express yourself authentically and embrace the journey of self-exploration. Allow your creativity to flow, and honor the insights that arise from your artistic endeavors.

Interview and Dialogue Exercises

Interview and dialogue exercises provide valuable opportunities for self-reflection, connection, and deeper understanding of gender identity and sexual orientation. Engaging in conversations with others—whether they are friends, family members, or even strangers—can foster empathy and create a supportive environment for exploration. These exercises also allow you to articulate your thoughts and feelings, helping to clarify your own identity in the process.

1. Personal Interview

Prompt: Conduct a personal interview with yourself, focusing on your experiences and feelings related to your gender identity and sexual orientation.

- Instructions: Set aside time in a quiet space to reflect and write down your answers to the following questions. Consider recording your responses in a journal or speaking them aloud to capture your thoughts authentically. Use the following pages to collect responses.

Sample Questions:

1. When did you first begin to question your gender identity or sexual orientation?

2. What experiences or events have shaped your understanding of yourself?

3. How do you feel about your identity today compared to when you first began exploring it?

4. What challenges have you faced in your journey of self-discovery?

5. Who or what has been most supportive in your exploration of your identity?

6. How do you envision your future self in relation to your gender identity and sexual orientation?

7. What affirmations or beliefs do you hold about your identity?

Collect Interview Transcript Below:

Reflection Questions:

- How did this exercise impact your understanding of your journey?

- Were there any insights or realizations that surprised you during the interview?

____
____
____
____
____
____
____
____
____
____

2. Interviewing Others

Prompt: Conduct an interview with someone close to you to explore their understanding of gender identity and sexual orientation.

- Instructions: Choose a friend, family member, or mentor who is open to discussing these topics. Prepare a set of questions in advance, and create a comfortable space for dialogue. Allow the person to share their thoughts and experiences freely, and be sure to listen actively. Collect interview transcript on the next page.

Sample Questions:

1. How do you define gender identity and sexual orientation?

2. Have you had any experiences that challenged or shaped your understanding of these concepts?

3. What are your thoughts on the importance of self-acceptance in relation to gender identity?

4. How can allies better support individuals exploring their identity?

5. What advice would you give to someone who is struggling with their gender identity or sexual orientation?

Collect Interview Transcript Here:

Reflection Questions:

- What did you learn from the person you interviewed?

- How did their experiences and insights resonate with your own journey?

____
____
____
____
____
____
____
____
____
____

3. Dialogue with an Imaginary Character

Prompt: Engage in a dialogue with an imaginary character who represents a different aspect of your identity or a figure who inspires you.

- Instructions: Choose a character—real or fictional—who embodies traits, beliefs, or experiences you wish to explore. Write a dialogue between yourself and this character, addressing topics related to gender identity and sexual orientation. Use the next page.

Sample Dialogue Starter:

- You: I've been struggling to accept my identity, and I often feel lost.

- Character: It's normal to feel lost at times. Embracing uncertainty can lead to growth. What specifically are you grappling with?

Collect Dialogue Below:

Reflection Questions:

- How did this dialogue help you explore different facets of your identity?

- What wisdom or guidance did your character offer that you can apply to your journey?

____

____

____

____

____

____

____

____

____

____

4. Group Discussion

Prompt: Organize a group discussion with peers or supportive individuals to share experiences and insights related to gender identity and sexual orientation.

- Instructions: Create a safe and respectful environment for participants to share their stories and perspectives. Establish ground rules for open communication, active listening, and confidentiality. Use guiding questions to facilitate discussion and encourage participation. Collect group discussion notes on the next page.

Sample Discussion Questions:

1. What does gender identity mean to you, and how has it evolved over time?

2. Can you share a moment when you felt truly accepted for who you are?

3. What challenges have you faced in your journey, and how have you overcome them?

4. How do you define allyship, and what actions can allies take to support individuals exploring their identity?

5. What resources or practices have helped you in your exploration?

Collect Group Discussion Notes Below:

Reflection Questions:

- How did participating in this group discussion affect your sense of belonging?

- What common themes or experiences emerged during the conversation?

____
____
____
____
____
____
____
____
____
____

5. Role-Playing Scenarios

Prompt: Engage in role-playing exercises to practice conversations related to gender identity and sexual orientation.

- Instructions: Choose scenarios that may arise in your life, such as coming out to a friend, discussing your identity with family members, or addressing misunderstandings about your gender identity. Work with a partner or group to act out these scenarios, focusing on communication and emotional expression. Collect these on the next page.

Sample Scenarios:

1. Coming out to a close friend who may not be familiar with LGBTQ+ topics.

2. Explaining your identity to family members who hold traditional beliefs.

3. Addressing questions or misconceptions in a supportive environment.

Write Scenarios Here:

1. ____
2. ____
3. ____
4. ____
5. ____
6. ____
7. ____
8. ____
9. ____
10. ____
11. ____
12. ____
13. ____
14. ____
15. ____
16. ____
17. ____
18. ____
19. ____
20. ____

Reflection Questions:

- How did role-playing these scenarios help you prepare for real-life conversations?

- What emotions surfaced during the exercises, and how did they influence your perspective?

____
____
____
____
____
____
____

Conclusion of Interview and Dialogue Exercises

Engaging in interview and dialogue exercises can be transformative as you navigate your journey of self-discovery. These activities provide a platform for exploration, connection, and understanding, enabling you to articulate your thoughts and feelings while gaining insights from others. Whether you are reflecting on your experiences, engaging in meaningful conversations, or practicing communication skills, these exercises can enhance your understanding of your gender identity and sexual orientation. Embrace the power of dialogue as a tool for growth, and honor the richness of your journey.

Goal-Setting for Identity Exploration

Setting goals can be an empowering way to navigate the journey of exploring your gender identity and sexual orientation. This process encourages self-reflection, intentionality, and commitment to personal growth. By establishing clear, achievable goals, you can create a roadmap that guides you through your exploration, helping you to stay focused and motivated while also providing a framework for measuring progress. In this section, we will outline the importance of goal-setting, introduce various types of goals, and provide strategies to help you articulate and pursue your identity exploration goals.

Importance of Goal-Setting

Goal-setting is crucial for several reasons:

1. Clarity and Focus: Setting specific goals helps clarify what you want to achieve, providing a sense of direction in your journey of self-exploration. This clarity allows you to prioritize your efforts and focus on activities that align with your identity.

2. Motivation and Accountability: Goals serve as a source of motivation, inspiring you to take actionable steps toward your desired outcomes. Writing down your goals can also create a sense of accountability, making it easier to track your progress and stay committed.

3. Empowerment: Establishing and achieving goals fosters a sense of empowerment, reinforcing the belief that you have the agency to shape your identity and experiences. Each goal you accomplish can boost your confidence and encourage you to set even more ambitious goals.

4. Reflection and Growth: The process of setting and reviewing your goals allows for continuous reflection and growth. Regularly assessing your progress can help you identify areas of strength and opportunities for further exploration, enabling you to adapt your goals as your understanding of your identity evolves.

Types of Goals for Identity Exploration

When it comes to exploring your gender identity and sexual orientation, goals can be categorized into several types:

1. Personal Reflection Goals:

 - Objective: Engage in self-discovery and self-reflection to deepen your understanding of your identity.

 - Example Goal: Spend 15 minutes each day journaling about your thoughts and feelings related to your gender identity for one month.

2. Educational Goals:

 - Objective: Increase your knowledge about gender identity and sexual orientation, including LGBTQ+ history, terminology, and resources.

 - Example Goal: Read three books or articles about gender identity and LGBTQ+ experiences over the next six weeks.

3. Community Engagement Goals:

 - Objective: Connect with others in the LGBTQ+ community to share experiences and build support networks.

 - Example Goal: Attend at least one LGBTQ+ community event or support group meeting per month.

4. Advocacy Goals:

 - Objective: Advocate for yourself and others within the LGBTQ+ community, promoting awareness and understanding.

 - Example Goal: Write a letter to a local representative advocating for LGBTQ+ rights within the next three months.

5. Creative Expression Goals:

 - Objective: Use creative outlets to explore and express your identity.

 - Example Goal: Create one piece of art, music, or writing that reflects your identity each month.

6. Social Interaction Goals:

 - Objective: Practice conversations and interactions related to your identity with friends, family, or allies.

 - Example Goal: Have an open conversation with one trusted friend or family member about your identity at least once a month.

Strategies for Setting Effective Goals

To create meaningful and achievable goals, consider using the SMART criteria, which can help ensure your goals are Specific, Measurable, Achievable, Relevant, and Time-bound.

1. Specific: Clearly define your goal. Instead of saying, I want to learn more about LGBTQ+ issues, you could specify, I want to read two books about gender identity by the end of the month.

2. Measurable: Establish criteria for measuring progress. This could include setting a specific number of resources to consume or activities to engage in.

3. Achievable: Ensure your goal is realistic and attainable within your current circumstances. If you have a busy schedule, setting a goal to read one article per week may be more achievable than committing to a book each week.

4. Relevant: Align your goals with your personal values and interests. Consider how each goal contributes to your journey of self-discovery and exploration of your identity.

5. Time-bound: Set a timeframe for achieving your goals. This can create a sense of urgency and help you stay committed.

Goal-Setting Worksheet

To assist you in articulating and tracking your goals, consider using the following worksheet:

Goal-Setting Worksheet

To assist you in articulating and tracking your goals, consider using the following worksheet:

Goal	Specific Action	Start Date	End Date	Progress/Notes

Conclusion of Goal-Setting for Identity Exploration

Goal-setting for identity exploration is a powerful way to take charge of your journey toward self-discovery. By establishing clear, intentional goals, you can create a structured approach to understanding your gender identity and sexual orientation. As you work through this process, remember to celebrate your achievements, no matter how small, and be gentle with yourself as you navigate the complexities of your identity. Your journey is unique, and each step you take is a testament to your courage and commitment to authenticity.

Resource Compilation for Specific Identities

As individuals navigate their journeys of exploring gender identity and sexual orientation, access to tailored resources can provide essential support, information, and community connection. This resource compilation is designed to address the unique needs and experiences of specific identities within the LGBTQ+ spectrum. Each section includes a variety of resources, including books, websites, organizations, and support networks, aimed at fostering understanding and empowerment.

1. Transgender and Non-Binary Identities

Books:

- Transgender History by Susan Stryker: A comprehensive overview of transgender history in the United States, highlighting key events and figures.

- The Gendered Self by Riki Wilchins: A thought-provoking exploration of gender identity and expression, challenging societal norms and expectations.

Websites:

- Transgender Network (www.transgendernetwork.org): A resource hub offering support, information, and community for transgender individuals.

- GLAAD's Transgender Resources (www.glaad.org/transgender): A guide to understanding transgender issues, terminology, and allyship.

Organizations:

- National Center for Transgender Equality (www.transequality.org): Advocates for transgender rights and provides resources on legal issues, healthcare, and public policy.

- Trans Lifeline (www.translifeline.org): A peer-support hotline offering crisis intervention and resources for transgender individuals.

2. Genderqueer and Gender Non-Conforming Identities

Books:

- Gender Outlaws: The Next Generation by Kate Bornstein and S. Bear Bergman: A collection of essays by gender non-conforming individuals exploring their experiences and identities.

- Beyond the Gender Binary by Alok Vaid-Menon: A powerful exploration of gender diversity, challenging binary perceptions of gender.

Websites:

- Gender Spectrum (www.genderspectrum.org): A resource for understanding and supporting gender diversity in youth and families.

- Nonbinary Wiki (www.nonbinary.wiki): A collaborative platform for sharing information and resources related to non-binary identities.

Organizations:

- Gender Justice (www.genderjustice.org): Advocates for the rights of gender non-conforming individuals and provides resources on legal protections and community support.

- The Trevor Project (www.thetrevorproject.org): A national organization offering crisis intervention and suicide prevention services for LGBTQ+ youth, including resources for non-binary individuals.

3. Bisexual and Pansexual Identities

Books:

- The Bisexual Option by Fred S. Berliner: A foundational text exploring bisexual identity and experiences, addressing misconceptions and challenges.

- Not Your Sidekick by C.B. Lee: A young adult novel featuring a bisexual protagonist navigating love, identity, and heroism.

Websites:

- Bi.org (www.bi.org): A comprehensive resource for bisexual individuals, providing information on community, advocacy, and events.

- Bi Visibility (www.bivisibility.com): A platform dedicated to raising awareness and celebrating bisexuality through education and community-building.

Organizations:

- American Institute of Bisexuality (www.bisexual.org): Promotes the visibility and understanding of bisexuality, offering resources and support for bisexual individuals.

- Bisexual Resource Center (www.biresource.net): Provides information, support, and advocacy for bisexual individuals and their allies.

4. Asexual and Aromantic Identities

Books:

- The Invisible Orientation: An Introduction to Asexuality by Julie Sondra Decker: A comprehensive guide to understanding asexuality, addressing misconceptions and providing support.

- Asexuality: A Brief Introduction by Anthony F. W. Decker: An accessible overview of asexuality, exploring the spectrum of sexual attraction and identity.

Websites:

- AVEN (Asexual Visibility and Education Network) (www.asexuality.org): A community-driven platform providing information and support for asexual individuals and allies.

- Aromantic Spectrum Network (www.arosupport.org): A resource hub for individuals identifying as aromantic, offering information, support, and community connections.

Organizations:

- Asexual Outreach (www.asexualoutreach.org): Advocates for asexual visibility and provides resources for individuals exploring asexuality.

- The Asexuality Archive (www.asexualarchive.com): A repository of academic research and personal narratives related to asexuality.

5. Intersex Identities

Books:

- Intersex (For Lack of a Better Word) by Thea Hillman: A memoir exploring the author's experiences as an intersex individual and the complexities of identity.

- Being Intersex: A Personal Story by Jodie M. O'Brien: A narrative reflecting on the author's journey of self-acceptance and advocacy.

Websites:

- Intersex Society of North America (www.isna.org): A resource dedicated to intersex advocacy, education, and support.

- InterACT (www.interactadvocates.org): An organization advocating for the rights and dignity of intersex individuals, providing resources and information.

Organizations:

- OII (Organization Intersex International) (www.oii.org): A global network advocating for intersex rights and providing resources for intersex individuals and their families.

- The Intersex Justice Project (www.intersexjustice.org): A project focused on advocacy and support for intersex individuals, promoting awareness and understanding.

6. LGBTQ+ Allies and Supporters

Books:

- The ABC's of LGBT+ by Ashley Mardell: A comprehensive guide to understanding LGBTQ+ identities and terminology, aimed at allies and supporters.

- Queer (In)Justice: The Criminalization of LGBT People in the United States by Joey L. Mogul, Andrea J. Ritchie, and Kay Whitlock: An exploration of the intersections between the LGBTQ+ community and the criminal justice system.

Websites:

- PFLAG (www.pflag.org): A national organization supporting LGBTQ+ individuals and their families through education, advocacy, and support groups.

- GLSEN (www.glsen.org): An organization dedicated to ensuring safe and affirming schools for LGBTQ+ youth, providing resources for educators and allies.

Organizations:

- Human Rights Campaign (www.hrc.org): Advocates for LGBTQ+ equality and provides resources for allies seeking to support the community.

- The Williams Institute (www.williamsinstitute.law.ucla.edu): A research center focused on LGBTQ+ issues, providing data and resources for advocacy.

Conclusion of Resource Compilation for Specific Identities

This resource compilation is intended to empower individuals exploring their gender identity and sexual orientation by providing access to relevant information, support networks, and community resources. Whether you are seeking personal reflection, community connection, or advocacy tools, these resources can serve as valuable tools on your journey of self-discovery. Remember, you are not alone in this exploration, and there are many resources available to support you in embracing your authentic self.

Journal Prompt:

- Who are the people in my life that I can turn to for support regarding my gender identity and sexual orientation?

- What qualities do I value in my support network, and how can I foster those relationships?

Real-Life Stories and Testimonials

Real-life stories and testimonials are powerful tools for understanding the diverse experiences of adults navigating their gender identity and sexual orientation. These narratives illustrate the complexities of self-discovery, the challenges faced, and the triumphs achieved along the journey. By sharing these stories, we can foster empathy, connection, and inspiration, creating a sense of community and support for those exploring their identities later in life.

Stories from Transgender and Non-Binary Adults

1. Jordan's Journey to Authenticity

- I spent decades feeling different but didn't have the language to express it until my forties when I discovered the concept of being non-binary. At first, it was difficult to come out to my family, but over time, they began to understand and support me. Now, I feel more myself than ever before. Embracing my identity at this stage in my life has been a journey of self-acceptance, and I'm proud of who I am.

2. Ava's Transition Story

- After years of feeling trapped in a body that didn't reflect who I was inside, I decided to come out as transgender in my late thirties. I remember the day I started hormone therapy; it felt like I was finally taking control of my life. I faced challenges, like losing friends and navigating societal expectations, but I also found an incredible community of support. My journey is ongoing, but each day I get closer to being my true self.

Stories from Bisexual and Pansexual Adults

1. Eli's Bisexual Revelation

- For a long time, I struggled with my bisexuality because I didn't see enough representation in media, especially for adults. I felt pressured to choose a side. When I finally embraced my identity in my fifties, I began connecting with other bisexual individuals and learned that my experiences were valid. I now proudly identify as bisexual and advocate for bisexual visibility. It's important for everyone to know that their identity is real, regardless of how others perceive it.

2. Sophia's Pansexual Pride

- Identifying as pansexual has been liberating, but it also comes with its challenges, especially as I navigate the expectations of those around me. Some people misunderstand what it means to be pansexual, thinking it's just a phase. However, I've learned to embrace my identity unapologetically. I love who I love, regardless of gender. Sharing my story has helped others feel more comfortable exploring their own identities, and I hope to continue fostering that acceptance.

Stories from Asexual and Aromantic Adults

1. Max's Asexual Journey

- As an adult, I always thought something was wrong with me because I wasn't interested in sex. Discovering the asexual community in my forties was a turning point. I realized I wasn't alone and that asexuality is a valid identity. It took time, but I learned to embrace my orientation and advocate for myself in relationships. I've formed close friendships with other asexual individuals who understand my experiences, which has been incredibly affirming.

2. Riley's Aromantic Experience

- I identify as aromantic, and for years, I felt pressured to conform to societal norms about love and relationships, especially as I entered my fifties. I didn't want a romantic relationship, and that was okay. Once I found the aromantic community, I felt accepted for who I am. I've learned to create fulfilling connections with friends and family that don't revolve around romance. My identity is valid, and I now celebrate the love I share with people in my life.

Stories from Intersex Adults

1. Jamie's Intersex Advocacy

- Growing up intersex, I often felt like I didn't fit in. Doctors tried to 'fix' me, subjecting me to unnecessary medical interventions without my consent. It wasn't until I connected with the intersex community as an adult that I found my voice. Now, I advocate for intersex rights, sharing my story to raise awareness about the importance of bodily autonomy. I want others to know they are not alone and that their bodies are their own to define.

2. Taylor's Journey of Acceptance

- As an intersex person in my sixties, my journey has been filled with self-discovery and acceptance. Initially, I felt ashamed of my differences, but over time, I learned to embrace my identity. By sharing my story with others, I've connected with people who understand my experiences. Advocacy work has been incredibly rewarding, and I strive to create a world where intersex individuals are respected and celebrated.

Quotes from LGBTQ+ Adults

1. Alex, a Non-Binary Activist:

- The journey to understanding my gender has been messy, beautiful, and transformative. I've learned that it's okay to take up space and to challenge societal norms. My identity is valid, and it deserves to be celebrated.

2. Sam, a Transgender Man:

- Transitioning in my forties has been the most challenging yet rewarding experience of my life. I've faced discrimination and obstacles, but I've also found incredible love and support in unexpected places. My journey is a testament to resilience and authenticity.

3. Taylor, a Bisexual Woman:

- Being bisexual means loving deeply and openly, regardless of gender. It's about recognizing that love knows no boundaries. I embrace my identity and advocate for visibility because we deserve to be seen and heard.

4. Morgan, an Asexual Individual:

- Asexuality is often misunderstood, but it's just as valid as any other orientation. I'm learning to embrace my identity and find joy in connections that aren't defined by sexual attraction.

Conclusion of Real-Life Stories and Testimonials

Real-life stories and testimonials from adults exploring their gender identity and sexual orientation provide valuable insight into the diverse experiences of self-discovery. These narratives highlight the importance of self-acceptance, community support, and the ongoing journey of understanding one's identity. By sharing their experiences, these individuals inspire others to embrace their authentic selves and advocate for visibility and understanding within the LGBTQ+ community. Each story serves as a reminder that every journey is unique, and together, we can create a more inclusive world for all.

Journal Prompt:

- What have I learned about myself through this exploration so far?

- Are there any past experiences that have shaped my understanding of gender and sexuality? How do they influence me today?

____
____
____

Future Visioning Exercises

Future visioning exercises are powerful tools that allow adults and older adults to envision their ideal selves and identities. These exercises promote introspection, creativity, and goal-setting, helping individuals articulate their aspirations, overcome fears, and foster a sense of empowerment as they navigate their gender identity and sexual orientation. The following activities encourage self-reflection and the imagination necessary to visualize a fulfilling and authentic future.

Exercise 1: Vision Board Creation

Purpose: This exercise helps individuals visually represent their dreams, aspirations, and the future they wish to create concerning their identity.

Instructions:

1. Gather materials such as magazines, scissors, glue, and a poster board or digital tools if preferred. You can also use the next page.

2. Take a moment to reflect on what an ideal future looks like for you regarding your gender identity and sexual orientation. Consider aspects such as:

   - Personal relationships

   - Career aspirations

   - Community involvement

   - Self-expression and style

3. Cut out images, words, and phrases from magazines or use digital images that resonate with your vision.

4. Arrange these cutouts on your poster board, creating a collage that represents your future.

5. Display your vision board in a prominent place to serve as a daily reminder of your aspirations.

Make Vision Board Here:

Journal on how this activity impacted you

____
____
____
____
____
____
____
____
____
____

Exercise 2: Guided Visualization

Purpose: This guided exercise helps individuals imagine their future self in a safe and supportive space.

Instructions:

1. Find a comfortable, quiet place to sit or lie down where you won't be disturbed.

2. Close your eyes and take a few deep breaths to center yourself.

3. Visualize a peaceful scene that makes you feel safe and relaxed.

4. As you settle into this visualization, begin to picture your future self—who you are, how you look, and how you carry yourself. Consider:

  - What clothes are you wearing?

  - How do you express your identity?

  - What relationships do you have in your life?

  - How do you feel about yourself?

5. Spend a few minutes in this visualization, allowing yourself to absorb the feelings and sensations of being your future self.

6. When you are ready, slowly return to the present moment and take a few deep breaths before opening your eyes. Write down your experiences and feelings in a journal.

Journal on How this activity impacted you

____
____
____
____
____
____
____
____
____
____
____

Exercise 3: Letter to Your Future Self

Purpose: This reflective writing exercise allows individuals to articulate their hopes, dreams, and goals for their future self.

Instructions:

1. Find a quiet space and gather your journaling materials, or use the next page.

2. Begin by addressing a letter to your future self. Start with Dear [Your Name], and set a date for when you want to read this letter (e.g., one year from now).

3. Write about your aspirations, including:

  - Your hopes for how you'll express your gender identity or sexual orientation.

  - Goals you want to achieve (e.g., coming out, joining a community group, or pursuing a relationship).

  - Challenges you anticipate and how you plan to overcome them.

  - Affirmations or encouraging statements you want to remind yourself of in the future.

4. Seal the letter in an envelope and keep it in a safe place until the date you set to read it. Reflect on your growth and the progress you've made since writing the letter.

Write Letter Here:

Journal on how this activity impacted you

____
____
____
____
____
____
____
____
____
____
____

Exercise 4: Creating Your Personal Mission Statement

Purpose: This exercise helps individuals clarify their values and priorities regarding their identity.

Instructions:

1. Take some time to reflect on the values that are most important to you, such as authenticity, community, love, or self-expression.

2. Write down a list of these core values on the next page.

3. Using these values as a foundation, draft a personal mission statement that captures your goals and intentions for your future regarding your gender identity and sexual orientation. Consider the following prompts:

  - What kind of person do you want to be in the future?

  - How do you want to relate to others?

  - What contributions do you want to make to your community?

4. Keep your mission statement somewhere visible to remind you of your goals and values as you move forward.

List of Core Values:

1. ____

2. ____

3. ____

4. ____

5. ____

6. ____

7. ____

8. ____

9. ____

10. ____

11. ____

12. ____

13. ____

14. ____

15. ____

16. ____

17. ____

18. ____

19. ____

20. ____

Journal on how this activity impacted you

____

____

____

____

____

____

____

____

Exercise 5: Future Identity Mapping

Purpose: This mapping exercise helps individuals visualize the steps needed to achieve their future identity goals.

Instructions:

1. Start by drawing a large circle in the center of the next paper. In this circle, write or draw your envisioned future identity (e.g., Proud Non-Binary Activist or Confident Transgender Person).

2. From this central circle, draw lines extending outward to smaller circles that represent specific goals or aspirations related to that identity. For example:

  - Building a supportive friend group

  - Seeking therapy or counseling

  - Advocating for LGBTQ+ rights

3. For each smaller circle, brainstorm actionable steps you can take to work towards these goals. Write these steps down as smaller branches extending from the goals.

4. Review your identity map regularly, adjusting and adding to it as your goals evolve.

Draw Future Identity Mapping Here:

Journal on how this activity impacted you

____
____
____
____
____
____
____
____
____
____

Reflection on Future Visioning Exercises

Engaging in future visioning exercises can be transformative for adults exploring their gender identity and sexual orientation. These activities encourage self-exploration and empower individuals to articulate their aspirations for the future. By creating a clear vision, adults can build the confidence and motivation needed to pursue their identities authentically and navigate their journeys with purpose.

Conclusion

The journey of self-exploration is complex and multifaceted. For many adults, it involves confronting societal expectations, internalized biases, and the fear of judgment from others. It is essential to recognize that this process is not linear; it may include moments of clarity, confusion, joy, and discomfort.

Section 2: Understanding Sexual Orientation

Defining Sexual Orientation

Understanding sexual orientation is a foundational aspect of exploring one's identity, particularly for adults and older adults who may be reassessing their lives and experiences. Sexual orientation refers to the emotional, romantic, or sexual attraction one feels toward people of the same or different genders. It encompasses a range of identities that reflect the diverse ways individuals relate to others.

This section will help you define and reflect on the various orientations within the LGBTQ+ spectrum, including:

- Heterosexual: Attraction to individuals of the opposite gender.

- Homosexual: Attraction to individuals of the same gender, often referred to as gay or lesbian.

- Bisexual: Attraction to individuals of more than one gender.

- Pansexual: Attraction to individuals regardless of their gender, focusing on the person rather than their gender identity.

- Asexual: A lack of sexual attraction to others, which can encompass a spectrum of experiences, including varying levels of romantic attraction.

- Queer: An umbrella term that encompasses a variety of sexual orientations and gender identities, often used to signify a non-normative stance toward sexuality.

- Questioning: A term for individuals who are exploring their sexual orientation and may not have settled on a specific identity yet.

1. Activity: Create a mind map on the next paper of different sexual orientations. Start with Sexual Orientation in the center, branching out to include the various orientations listed above. For each orientation, add sub-branches to explore:

- Characteristics: What defines this orientation?

- Common Experiences: What are some common feelings or experiences associated with this orientation?

- Personal Resonance: Reflect on how each orientation resonates with your feelings or experiences. Are there orientations you identify with or have questions about?

Make Mind Map Here:

Engaging in this activity encourages you to explore the rich tapestry of sexual orientations and helps you understand where you might fit within this spectrum.

Journaling Prompt: Reflect on what sexual orientation means to you. Consider your understanding of the different orientations you identified in your mind map. Write about your own orientation and how you identify. Think about your journey and any shifts in your understanding of your sexual orientation over time. Have there been influences from culture, family, or personal experiences that have shaped your perspective?

2. Exploring Attraction

Attraction is a complex and multifaceted experience that can encompass emotional, physical, and romantic dimensions. Understanding how these forms of attraction relate to your sexual orientation can provide deeper insights into your identity and relationships. As adults, it's common to experience nuanced attractions that may not fit neatly into traditional categories, and exploring these can enhance self-awareness.

Activity: Reflect on the different kinds of attraction you experience by creating a chart on the next page with three main categories:

- Emotional Attraction:

  - Who do you feel emotionally drawn to?

  - What qualities or traits do you appreciate in these individuals?

  - Write down experiences where emotional attraction has played a significant role in your relationships.

- Physical Attraction:

  - List individuals you find physically appealing, considering both current and past attractions.

  - Note any patterns, such as recurring traits or types you are drawn to.

  - Reflect on how physical attraction has influenced your experiences in dating or relationships.

- Romantic Attraction:

  - Reflect on your romantic connections and who you feel romantically linked to.

  - Consider how romantic attraction influences your desires for intimacy, commitment, or companionship.

  - Write about moments where romantic attraction has guided your actions or decisions.

This chart serves as a tool to visualize the different dimensions of your attractions, allowing you to understand how they may intersect with your sexual orientation.

Emotional Attraction	Physical Attraction	Romantic Attraction

Journaling Prompt: Describe your experiences with attraction in detail. Reflect on how these experiences relate to your sexual orientation. Consider the nuances of your attractions—do you experience them differently based on gender or the type of relationship? Explore how these attractions shape your self-perception and your interactions with others. Are there challenges or joys you've encountered in navigating these attractions?

____
____
____
____
____
____
____
____
____
____
____

3. Identifying Your Sexual Orientation

Identifying your sexual orientation can be a deeply personal journey that involves reflection on your feelings, relationships, and attractions. For established adults and older adults, this exploration may bring up both excitement and apprehension, especially if societal norms have historically influenced how they perceive their identities. Understanding your sexual orientation requires a commitment to self-exploration and honesty.

Activity: To help clarify your sexual orientation, answer the following questions thoughtfully:

- What feelings do you have toward individuals of various genders? Describe any specific individuals or relationships that stand out.

- Have you had romantic relationships? If so, what patterns do you notice regarding the genders of your partners and the nature of these relationships?

- How do your attractions impact your identity and self-perception? Reflect on how identifying with a particular orientation influences your day-to-day life, relationships, and sense of community.

____
____
____
____
____
____
____
____

Once you've answered these questions, consider how your responses align with the definitions and categories discussed earlier. This reflection may help clarify your understanding of your sexual orientation.

Journaling Prompt: Write a narrative about your journey of discovering your sexual orientation. Include key moments, experiences, or realizations that have shaped your understanding of who you are. Reflect on the emotions you felt during this journey—were there challenges you faced, and how did you overcome them? How has your understanding of your orientation evolved over time, and what support systems have been beneficial in this process?

____
____
____
____
____
____
____
____
____
____
____

Theories of Sexual Orientation Development

There are many theories of sexual orientation development, and the following theories are meant to validate the journey of discovering sexual orientation, and as a jumping off point for you to research more on your own. The Human Development Model is a Model of Lesbian, Gay, and Bisexual Identity Development. This model, developed by Anthony D'Augelli, is a life-span approach to understanding sexual orientation identity development. Unlike stage models that suggest a linear progression, D'Augelli's model emphasizes that identity development is a fluid and ongoing process influenced by social, cultural, and environmental factors. The model outlines six interactive processes rather than steps or stages. Here they are:

1.   Exiting Heterosexual Identity   : This process involves recognizing and coming to terms with one's sexual orientation as different from the heterosexual norm. Individuals begin to acknowledge that they are lesbian, gay, or bisexual and start to distance themselves from a heterosexual identity.

2.   Developing a Personal LGB Identity Status   : In this process, individuals work to develop a positive self-concept as a lesbian, gay, or bisexual person. This involves managing internalized homophobia, coming to terms with one's sexual orientation, and building a positive LGB identity.

3.   Developing a LGB Social Identity   : Here, individuals start to seek out and connect with other LGB people and communities. This process is about finding social support and creating a sense of belonging within the LGB community.

4.   Becoming a LGB Offspring   : This process involves coming out to family members, particularly parents. It's about navigating the complexities of family relationships and negotiating acceptance or rejection based on one's sexual orientation.

5.   Developing a LGB Intimacy Status   : In this process, individuals work on forming intimate relationships with partners, which includes developing skills for maintaining healthy and fulfilling relationships in the context of their sexual orientation.

6.   Entering a LGB Community   : Finally, individuals become more involved in the broader LGB community, often engaging in advocacy or community-building efforts. This process can involve participating in LGB organizations, activism, or other community activities.

D'Augelli's model highlights the non-linear and ongoing nature of identity development, taking into account the broader social and cultural contexts that influence an individual's experience as they navigate their sexual orientation throughout life.

Ecological Model of Gay Male Development

The Ecological Model of Gay Male Development, developed by Urie Bronfenbrenner, considers the complex interactions between an individual and their environment in the process of gay male identity development. This model emphasizes the role of multiple levels of influence, including personal factors (such as internalized homophobia), relational factors (such as support from friends and family), community factors (such as the presence of a supportive gay community), and societal factors (such as legal rights and cultural acceptance). The steps in this model involve navigating these various influences, often beginning with internal awareness of one's sexual orientation, seeking out supportive environments, forming a gay identity within a community context, and ultimately integrating this identity into broader society.

1.   Microsystem   : This is the immediate environment where the individual interacts directly, such as family, friends, school, and work. In the context of gay male development, the support or rejection from family members, acceptance by peers, and experiences in educational settings are crucial.

2.   Mesosystem   : This level involves the interactions between different microsystems, such as the relationship between family and school or peer groups and work. For gay men, the connections between different aspects of their social world (e.g., how family attitudes affect school experiences) are important in shaping their identity.

3.   Exosystem   : This includes broader social systems that indirectly influence the individual, such as community, neighborhood, and media. For example, the presence of LGBT+ representation in media or community support services can significantly impact a gay man's development.

4.   Macrosystem   : The macrosystem encompasses cultural values, laws, and societal norms. The broader cultural attitudes toward homosexuality, legal rights, and societal acceptance or discrimination play a key role in the development of a gay male identity.

5.   Chronosystem   : This refers to the dimension of time, including life transitions and historical contexts. Significant life events, such as coming out, changes in legal status, or shifts in societal attitudes, and the historical context in which an individual lives, affect identity development over time.

Lesbian and Socially Oriented Models

Lesbian and socially oriented models, developed by Adrienne Rich, focus on the development of sexual identity within a social and cultural context. These models often highlight the unique challenges faced by lesbians, including the impact of sexism and heteronormativity. Steps in these models typically include awareness of same-sex attraction, seeking out supportive communities, developing a positive lesbian identity, and integrating this identity into one's overall sense of self. Socially oriented models emphasize the importance of community and relationships in this process, recognizing that lesbian identity is shaped not only by personal experiences but also by the social environments in which individuals live.

Lesbian and socially oriented models of identity development often emphasize the interplay between individual identity and social context, focusing on how societal factors influence the process. While there isn't a single, universally accepted model, a few influential frameworks and concepts have been developed. Below are steps based on common themes in these models:

1.   Awareness of Same-Sex Attraction   :

   - The individual begins to recognize feelings of attraction toward people of the same sex. This awareness may be gradual and often occurs in the context of a heteronormative society.

 2.   Exploration of Lesbian Identity   :

- The individual starts to explore what it means to be a lesbian, seeking information, resources, and potentially engaging with lesbian communities. This stage often involves questioning societal norms and considering one's place within them.

3.   Disclosure and Coming Out   :

- The process of coming out to oneself and others begins. This involves sharing one's sexual orientation with friends, family, and potentially more broadly. The individual navigates acceptance or rejection from these social circles.

4.   Identity Integration   :

- The individual integrates their lesbian identity with other aspects of their life and self. They develop a positive self-concept as a lesbian, finding ways to reconcile their identity with their personal values, beliefs, and other social roles.

5.   Formation of Intimate Relationships   :

- Developing and maintaining intimate, romantic, and sexual relationships with other women becomes a key aspect of this stage. The individual learns to navigate the dynamics of these relationships within the context of societal attitudes toward lesbian relationships.

6.   Community Involvement and Activism   :

- The individual may become more involved in lesbian and LGBTQ+ communities, engaging in activism or advocacy. This stage often reflects a commitment to challenging social norms and advocating for rights and acceptance.

Socially Oriented Models:

Socially oriented models, such as Adrienne Rich's concept of Compulsory Heterosexuality and the Lesbian Continuum , emphasize the social pressures that enforce heterosexuality and the broad spectrum of lesbian experiences and relationships. These models focus on the influence of societal structures on personal identity and the importance of creating and maintaining supportive communities.

Conclusion

By engaging with these activities and prompts, you can deepen your understanding of your sexual orientation while fostering a sense of community and connection with your identity. This section serves as a valuable resource for individuals on their journey to embrace their authentic selves.

Section 3: Intersectionality and Identity

Exploring Intersectionality

Intersectionality is a concept that recognizes the interconnected nature of various social identities, including race, gender, sexual orientation, class, and other categories. For adults and older adults, understanding intersectionality is vital in exploring how these overlapping identities influence experiences, challenges, and perspectives. The term was coined by scholar Kimberlé Crenshaw, emphasizing that individuals are not defined by a single identity but by the complex interplay of multiple identities.

In the context of gender identity and sexual orientation, intersectionality provides a framework for examining how various aspects of one's identity can shape experiences and outcomes. For instance, a queer individual of color may face different societal challenges than a heterosexual person from the same racial background. Recognizing these nuances helps individuals navigate their identities and fosters a deeper understanding of systemic inequalities.

1. Activity: Create a Venn diagram on the next page to explore how various aspects of your identity intersect with your gender identity and sexual orientation. Begin by drawing three overlapping circles. Label each circle with different aspects of your identity, such as:

- Gender Identity: Consider how you identify in relation to gender (e.g., woman, man, non-binary).

- Sexual Orientation: Reflect on your sexual orientation and how it relates to your gender identity.

- Other Aspects: Include additional identity factors such as race, ethnicity, socio-economic status, religion, age, and ability.

In the overlapping sections of the Venn diagram, write down how these aspects intersect with one another. For example, consider how being a queer person of a specific racial background may affect your experiences differently than those of a white queer individual. Reflect on the unique challenges and privileges that arise from these intersections.

Draw Your Venn Diagram Here:

Journaling Prompt: After completing your Venn diagram, take time to reflect on how these intersections impact your experiences and self-perception. Consider questions such as:

- In what ways do your intersecting identities enrich your life?

- Are there challenges you face that stem from the intersection of your identities?

- How do societal expectations regarding your race, gender, or sexual orientation influence how you perceive yourself and how others perceive you?

- Reflect on any internalized messages you may have received regarding your intersecting identities. How do these impact your sense of self-worth and belonging?

____
____
____
____
____
____
____
____
____
____

Cultural Influences

Cultural background plays a significant role in shaping our understanding of gender and sexuality. Each culture has its own beliefs, norms, and values surrounding these topics, which can influence how individuals experience and express their identities. For adults and older adults, exploring cultural influences can lead to greater self-awareness and understanding of how cultural narratives may have shaped their experiences throughout life.

Understanding cultural influences allows individuals to critically assess the messages they received growing up and how these messages align or conflict with their personal experiences. It opens the door to examining the intersectionality of culture with gender and sexual orientation, revealing the complex layers that inform one's identity.

1. Activity: Research and reflect on how your cultural background influences your understanding of gender and sexuality. Collect notes on the next page. Begin by identifying your cultural heritage and any specific cultural beliefs regarding gender and sexuality that you encountered during your upbringing. Consider using the following steps:

1. Research: Explore literature, articles, or online resources that discuss your cultural background's perspectives on gender and sexuality. Look for historical contexts, traditional beliefs, and any shifts that may have occurred over time.

2. Reflection: Write down key findings from your research, focusing on how these cultural perspectives align with or differ from your personal beliefs and experiences.

3. Cultural Artifacts: If possible, collect cultural artifacts (e.g., images, quotes, folklore, traditions) that reflect your cultural beliefs regarding gender and sexuality. Consider how these artifacts resonate with your own journey.

Collect Notes Here:

Journaling Prompt: After conducting your research, reflect on the messages you received about gender and sexuality while growing up. Consider the following prompts:

- What specific messages were communicated to you regarding gender roles and sexual orientation?

- Were there any influential figures (family, friends, community leaders) who shaped your understanding of these concepts?

- How do these cultural messages affect your understanding of your own identity today?

- Are there any cultural beliefs you have rejected, adopted, or redefined as you've grown older?

- Reflect on how your cultural background interacts with your current experiences of gender and sexuality. Do you find it empowering, challenging, or both?

____
____
____
____
____
____
____
____
____
____
____

Conclusion

By engaging in these activities and reflections, you can gain a deeper understanding of how intersectionality and cultural influences shape your identity. This section aims to encourage meaningful exploration of your experiences as you navigate the complexities of gender identity and sexual orientation.

Section 4: Personal Reflection and Growth

Self-Compassion and Acceptance

Self-compassion and acceptance are vital components of personal growth, particularly when exploring gender identity and sexual orientation. This process can evoke a wide range of emotions, including joy, confusion, and fear. For established adults and older adults, these feelings may be compounded by societal pressures, personal experiences, and cultural narratives. Practicing self-compassion involves treating oneself with kindness and understanding during difficult times, recognizing that everyone makes mistakes, and embracing the complexities of one's identity.

1. Activity: Write a letter to your past self on the next page, offering compassion and understanding regarding your journey. Start by addressing your past self with a warm greeting. Reflect on significant moments in your life that shaped your understanding of your identity, whether they were challenging or empowering. Include the following elements in your letter:

- Acknowledgment: Recognize the struggles and challenges your past self faced. Validate those feelings and experiences.

- Compassion: Offer words of comfort and understanding, acknowledging that it's okay to feel lost or unsure.

- Encouragement: Highlight the strengths you have developed over time. Remind your past self that growth is a journey and that it's important to embrace one's identity without fear of judgment.

- Affirmation: End your letter with affirmations of self-worth, reminding yourself of your value and the beauty of your journey.

This exercise encourages you to cultivate self-compassion and to recognize the resilience you possess.

Write Letter to Past Self Here:

Journaling Prompt: After writing your letter, reflect on what you have learned about self-acceptance and compassion through this exploration. Consider the following questions:

- How do your past experiences shape your understanding of self-compassion today?

- What barriers do you encounter when practicing self-acceptance?

- How can you integrate self-compassion into your daily life as you continue to explore your identity?

- In what ways can embracing self-acceptance impact your relationships and interactions with others?

____
____
____
____
____
____
____
____
____
____
____
____

Setting Goals for Personal Growth

Goal-setting is an essential step in the journey of personal reflection and growth. For adults and older adults exploring their gender identity and sexual orientation, setting specific, attainable goals can provide clarity and direction. These goals can be related to various aspects of your identity, including building community connections, engaging in educational pursuits, or exploring relationships.

1. Activity: Create a list of goals on the next page related to your gender identity and sexual orientation. Start by brainstorming various areas you wish to focus on. Consider goals that may include, but are not limited to:

- Finding a Supportive Community: Seek out local LGBTQ+ groups, online forums, or support networks that resonate with you.

- Educating Others: Set goals around educating friends, family, or colleagues about LGBTQ+ issues and your personal experiences.

- Exploring New Relationships: Identify goals related to dating, forming friendships, or deepening existing relationships.

- Personal Development: Consider goals centered on personal skills, such as assertiveness, communication, or self-expression.

List Goals Here:

1. ____

2. ____

3. ____

4. ____

5. ____

6. ____

7. ____

8. ____

9. ____

10. ____

11. ____

12. ____

13. ____

14. ____

15. ____

16. ____

17. ____

18. ____

19. ____

20. ____

Once you have created your list, prioritize your goals and break them down into actionable steps on the next page. For each goal, consider the following:

- What specific actions can you take to achieve this goal?

- What timeline do you envision for completing each goal?

- Are there potential obstacles you might face, and how can you address them?

List of Actions Related to Each Goal:

1. ____
2. ____
3. ____
4. ____
5. ____
6. ____
7. ____
8. ____
9. ____
10. ____
11. ____
12. ____
13. ____
14. ____
15. ____
16. ____
17. ____
18. ____
19. ____
20. ____

Journaling Prompt: Reflect on how you plan to achieve these goals. What resources or support do you need? Consider questions such as:

- What external resources (books, workshops, mentorship) can assist you in reaching your goals?

- Who in your life can provide support and encouragement on this journey?

- How will achieving these goals impact your sense of self and your relationships with others?

- What steps will you take to hold yourself accountable for your personal growth journey?

Celebrating Your Identity

Celebrating your identity is a powerful way to acknowledge and embrace who you are. For established adults and older adults, taking the time to honor one's gender identity and sexual orientation can be a transformative experience that fosters pride and self-acceptance. This celebration can manifest in various forms, from personal rituals to public affirmations.

1. Activity: Create a vision board that represents your gender identity and sexual orientation. Gather materials such as magazines, colored paper, scissors, and glue, and use the next page. Follow these steps:

1. Reflection: Begin by reflecting on symbols, words, and images that resonate with your identity. Consider what aspects of your identity you wish to celebrate and highlight.

2. Collecting Materials: Look for images, quotes, or symbols that reflect your journey and aspirations. This may include representations of pride, community, love, and self-acceptance.

3. Creating the Vision Board: Arrange the collected items on your board in a way that feels meaningful to you. There is no right or wrong way to do this—allow your creativity to flow.

4. Display: Once completed, find a place to display your vision board where you can see it regularly. This visual reminder can serve as an affirmation of your identity and your journey.

Make Collage Here:

Journaling Prompt: Write about what celebrating your identity means to you and how you plan to honor it in your life. Consider questions such as:

- How does embracing and celebrating your identity impact your mental and emotional well-being?

- What actions can you take to honor your identity regularly, whether through self-expression, community involvement, or personal rituals?

- How can you inspire others to celebrate their identities in a similar way?

- What steps can you take to create a more inclusive environment for others who may be exploring their identities?

____
____
____
____
____
____
____
____
____
____

Conclusion

Engaging with these activities and reflections in Section 4 allows for profound personal growth and self-acceptance. This section serves as a reminder that the journey of exploring gender identity and sexual orientation is ongoing, and celebrating who you are can lead to greater resilience and fulfillment.

Conclusion of the Workbook

Embarking on the journey to explore gender identity and sexual orientation can feel daunting, particularly for established adults who may have navigated life under rigid societal expectations. This process requires courage, vulnerability, and often a re-examination of long-held beliefs about oneself and the world. This workbook has been designed to facilitate that exploration, providing a structured yet flexible framework to help individuals engage deeply with their thoughts, feelings, and experiences.

One of the most significant challenges faced by adults in this exploration is the fear of judgment or rejection from others. Many individuals may find themselves grappling with concerns about how their evolving identities will impact their relationships, careers, or social standing. It's important to remember that this journey is uniquely yours, and the only expectations that matter are those you set for yourself. By using this workbook, you are taking a proactive step toward self-discovery and self-acceptance, prioritizing your well-being over the fears of external validation.

Throughout this workbook, you've encountered various activities and reflections designed to provoke thought and encourage honest self-expression. Each prompt is an invitation to dig deeper into your experiences, beliefs, and desires. This work may bring up uncomfortable feelings, but leaning into those emotions can lead to profound insights and a greater understanding of who you are at your core. It is essential to honor this process, allowing yourself the grace to feel, reflect, and grow without rushing to find immediate answers.

Moreover, engaging with the resources provided can enhance your understanding of the broader context surrounding gender identity and sexual orientation. Whether it's through literature, podcasts, or community events, these tools can enrich your journey by connecting you with a wealth of knowledge and diverse perspectives. Finding like-minded individuals who resonate with your experiences can foster a sense of belonging, reminding you that you are not alone in this journey. Building a supportive network can also provide essential encouragement and validation as you navigate this complex landscape.

In recognizing the importance of self-compassion, it's vital to be gentle with yourself as you explore your identity. The journey of self-discovery is rarely linear; it often involves twists, turns, and unexpected revelations. Embrace the uncertainties and trust that each step—no matter how small—contributes to your overall growth and understanding. Acknowledge your progress, celebrate your insights, and remind yourself that self-exploration is an ongoing process.

As you close this workbook, take a moment to reflect on the journey you've embarked upon. What have you learned about yourself? What new questions have arisen? The exploration of your gender identity and sexual orientation is a lifelong endeavor, one that will continue to evolve as you grow and change. Hold onto the insights gained here, and let them serve as a foundation for further exploration and self-affirmation.

In summary, this workbook is a catalyst for personal growth and self-discovery. It is an invitation to embrace your authentic self, challenge societal norms, and connect with a supportive community. As you continue this journey, remember that your voice matters, your experiences are valid, and your identity is worthy of celebration. Step forward with confidence and pride, knowing that you are forging a path toward a more authentic and fulfilling life.

Additional Resources

Here are additional resources to learn more about exploring your queer identity. Please see "Affirmations and Support Resources" if you are seeking resources to support you with overwhelming, negative feelings. If you are having thoughts of hurting yourself or someone else, call 911 or go to the nearest emergency room.

1. Books

- The Queer Bible Commentary edited by Christopher Steffen

  A comprehensive commentary that offers LGBTQ+ perspectives on biblical texts, ideal for individuals seeking to reconcile faith and identity.

- Trans Bodies, Trans Selves: A Resource for the Transgender Community edited by Laura Erickson-Schroth

  An essential resource that provides information on various aspects of life for transgender and gender nonconforming individuals.

- You Don't Have to Be a Housewife: A Guide to Life for the Modern Woman by Judith Levine

  This book challenges traditional gender roles and offers insights on navigating identity as a woman in contemporary society.

- Beyond the Gender Binary by Alok Vaid-Menon

  An exploration of gender beyond the binary framework, encouraging readers to embrace fluidity and diversity in gender identity.

2. Podcasts

- Identity Politics

  A podcast that examines identity through the lens of politics, culture, and personal narratives, featuring discussions on gender and sexual orientation.

- The Grown-Up Gays Podcast

  A podcast where hosts discuss various topics related to being an adult in the LGBTQ+ community, offering humor and insights.

- The LGBTQ+ Advocate

 Focuses on advocacy and community-building within the LGBTQ+ space, featuring guests who share their journeys and experiences.

3. Websites and Online Resources

- The National LGBTQ Task Force

 An advocacy organization that works towards advancing full freedom, justice, and equality for LGBTQ+ individuals.

 www.thetaskforce.org

- LGBTQ+ Resources by the Center for American Progress

 Offers research, reports, and policy analysis on LGBTQ+ issues, including those related to health, education, and legal rights.

 www.americanprogress.org

- OutRight Action International

 An organization that promotes and protects the human rights of LGBTQ+ people around the world, providing resources and advocacy tools.

 www.outrightinternational.org

4. Support Groups and Counseling Services

- Online Therapy Platforms

 Platforms like BetterHelp and Talkspace offer virtual therapy sessions with professionals who specialize in LGBTQ+ issues, providing accessible support.

- Adult LGBTQ+ Retreats

 Organizations such as Camp Brave Trails offer retreats designed for adults seeking connection and personal growth in an affirming environment.

5. Educational Resources

- The Gender Spectrum

An organization providing resources and training on gender diversity, focusing on education and advocacy for individuals and communities.

  www.genderspectrum.org

- Transgender Europe (TGEU)

  A European organization advocating for transgender rights, providing resources and information on issues affecting transgender individuals across Europe.

  www.tgeu.org

6. Workshops and Events

- LGBTQ+ Professional Development Workshops

  Many organizations offer professional development opportunities focused on LGBTQ+ issues in the workplace, promoting inclusivity and understanding.

- Local Book Clubs or Discussion Groups

  Consider joining or forming book clubs that focus on LGBTQ+ literature, creating a space for discussion and community engagement.

7. Affirming Apps and Online Tools

- Meetup

  A platform that connects individuals with similar interests, including LGBTQ+ groups and events in various communities.

- Happify

  An app designed to improve emotional health through activities and games, which can help individuals focus on positive self-reflection and personal growth.

8. Find a therapist to continue your understanding of yourself! Great tools to find therapists include calling your insurance to see which providers are covered in your area, or looking up providers on www.PsychologyToday.com

If you are looking to learn more from the author or need individualized support, please reach out to Christa McCrorie, LICSW-S, at:

Creative Therapeutic Solutions, LLC

PO Box 360763, Hoover, AL 35236

Phone: (205) 578-2692

christa.mccrorie@therapysecure.com

https://creativetherapeutic.solutions/

www.ingramcontent.com/pod-product-compliance
Lightning Source LLC
Chambersburg PA
CBHW081940160726
47999CB00008B/2463